100 Unforgettable Moments in
Pro Basketball

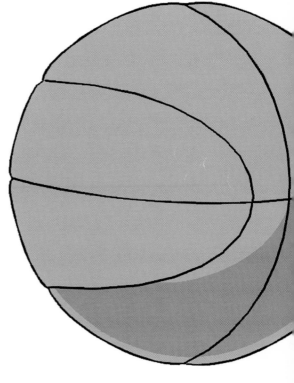

Bob Italia

ABDO & Daughters
Publishing

Published by Abdo & Daughters, 4940 Viking Drive,
Suite 622, Edina, Minnesota 55435.

Copyright © 1997 by Abdo Consulting Group, Inc.,
Pentagon Tower, P.O. Box 36036, Minneapolis, Minnesota
55435 USA. International copyrights reserved in all
countries. No part of this book may be reproduced in any
form without written permission from the publisher.

Printed in the United States.

Cover Photo credits: Allsport
Interior Photo credits: Wide World Photo

Edited by Paul Joseph

Library of Congress Cataloging-in-Publication Data

Italia, Bob, 1955-
  100 unforgettable moments in pro basketball / Bob Italia.
    p. cm. -- (100 unforgettable moments in sports)
Includes index.
Summary: Highlights major events in the history of the
sport of basketball, from the game's invention in 1891
through hundred-plus years of individual and team
records.
  ISBN 1-56239-692-7
1. Basketball--History--Juvenile literature. [1. Basketball-
History.] I. Title. II. Series: Italia, Bob, 1955- 100
unforgettable moments in sports. GV885.1.I83 1996
796.323'2--dc20
                          96-15014
                            CIP
                             AC

Contents

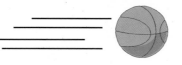

The Most Unforgettable Moment?

Since its formation in 1949, the National Basketball Association (NBA) has had many unforgettable moments, like Wilt Chamberlain's incredible 100-point game, or David Robinson's 71-point effort to win the 1994 scoring title.

Many unforgettable "moments" weren't moments at all. They took a season—or a career—to accomplish, like Boston's 8-consecutive NBA titles, Kareem Abdul-Jabbar's 38,387 career points, or Michael Jordan's 7-consecutive scoring championships.

There is no one most unforgettable moment in pro basketball history. The following stories are in chronological order, not according to importance. That judgment must be left up to basketball fans whose enthusiasm for this highly skilled sport has made it FAN-tastic!

Opposite page:
Kareem Abdul-Jabbar
and the sky-hook.

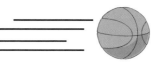

Dr. Naismith Invents Basketball

In 1891, in a YMCA in Springfield, Massachusetts, a young instructor named James Naismith invented a simple game in which players could test all of their athletic skills.

Naismith asked a custodian to nail two peach baskets to the gymnasium balcony. He wanted the elevated baskets to help promote athletic skills that football did not offer. But while basketball has always been a physical game, its 10-foot high hoop has enabled it to evolve into a showcase for great athletes to perform aerial acrobatics about which Dr. Naismith could only have dreamed.

Naismith did not foresee what the likes of Michael Jordan, Shaquille O'Neal, David Robinson, Hakeem Olajuwon, or Scottie Pippen would do to his simple, elegant game. Nor did he envision the huge, modern sports stadiums that would showcase the aerial acrobatics these great athletes could perform. All he wanted was an indoor activity for his students to play during the long New England winters. And it all started with two peach baskets.

James Naismith, the inventor of basketball.

Mikan Changes the Game

In 1948, the Minneapolis Lakers introduced a player who would become the sport's first superstar—and the first in a long history of great big men. His name was George Mikan.

At 6 feet, 10 inches tall and 245 pounds, the imposing Mikan changed the game forever with his dominating inside scoring. He was the first to use the hook shot to perfection. He also posted a 28.9 points per game average that earned him the first of three league-scoring titles.

To compete against the Lakers, opponents scrambled to find their own big players who could challenge Mikan and stop his relentless scoring. By the time these big players developed the skills necessary to compete with Mikan, he and his teammates had already established the first NBA dynasty.

George Mikan played for the Minneapolis Lakers.

The Birth of the NBA

In the summer of 1949, the six National Basketball League (NBL) teams joined the Basketball Association of America (BAA). The newly-formed league was renamed the National Basketball Association.

The NBA split into Eastern, Central, and Western divisions. Syracuse, the only NBL team in the East, won their division behind the play of big man Dolph Schayes, who averaged 16.8 points per game (ppg). Alex Groza averaged 23.4 for a new Indianapolis team that won the West, while George Mikan led the league with 27.4 ppg and helped the Minneapolis Lakers win the Central Division.

With three divisions, the playoff structure was a mess. Minneapolis had to beat Chicago, Fort Wayne, and Anderson to reach the Finals. Syracuse, however, had to defeat only Philadelphia and New York to qualify for the title round.

Syracuse had talented players like Schayes, Al Cervi, and Paul Seymour. But none could handle the dominating Mikan. Surrounded by other stars like Pollard, Martin, Harrison, and powerful Vern Mikkelsen, Mikan led the Lakers to their second-straight title with a six-game series victory.

Dolph Schayes averaged 16.8 points per game.

Three in a Row

In 1953, the NBA was still struggling to establish itself. Indianapolis folded, leaving the Western Division with only four teams—three of which would make the playoffs.

Neil Johnston averaged a league-leading 24.4 points per game, and Bob Cousy finished second at 19.2 ppg. He also led the league in assists with 7.2 per game.

George Mikan, now 30 years old, was playing fewer minutes as the Lakers tried to save him for the playoffs. He still averaged 18.1 points and 14.3 rebounds per game.

The playoffs began with a mini-tournament. The top three teams in each division played each other to see which two would advance. Syracuse won the East, ending New York's string of NBA Finals appearances. Minneapolis again won the West.

In their last championship game in Minneapolis, the Lakers won a tough Game 7, 87-80. With the victory, Minneapolis became the first NBA team to win three consecutive championships—and earned the honor of claiming the first basketball dynasty.

George Mikan of the Minneapolis Lakers comes up with a rebound against New York.

Elgin Baylor Arrives

In 1958, a new superstar burst on the NBA scene in Minneapolis who would raise the level of play to new heights. His name was Elgin Baylor. The 6-foot 5-inch rookie forward helped the Lakers go from a 19-53 record to a 33-39 record and a playoff berth by averaging 24.9 points and 15 rebounds per game. He also had a 55-point game—the third-highest in NBA history—and made the All-NBA team.

Baylor's athleticism was ahead of his time. His ability to leap and hang in the air set the standard for future stars like Connie Hawkins, Julius Erving, and Michael Jordan. Even more, his scoring ability signaled the beginning of a high-scoring era in the NBA. Big players with great athletic skills would now dominate the league. Elgin Baylor showed them how.

Opposite page: Elgin Baylor (dark uniform) goes for an NBA scoring title against the Knickerbockers.

1960

The 7-Foot 1-Inch Rookie

The NBA had seen dominating big men before—most notably George Mikan. But no one had ever seen the likes of Wilt Chamberlain. The rookie center for the Philadelphia Warriors stood 7-feet 1-inch tall and weighed 275 pounds. He towered over his closest rival, center Bill Russell of the Boston Celtics. Even worse for opponents, he seemed like a man amongst boys.

Chamberlain won both the Rookie of the Year and Most Valuable Player Awards. He led the league in scoring with a 37.6 average and in rebounding with a 27.0 average. Chamberlain scored 50 or more points 7 times. His team improved from a 32-40 record to a 49-26 record.

Never had the NBA seen such an explosive and dominating rookie. Impressive as his first-year statistics were, Chamberlain was just warming up.

Opposite page: Wilt Chamberlain (13) of the Philadelphia Warriors brings down a rebound against the Celtics.

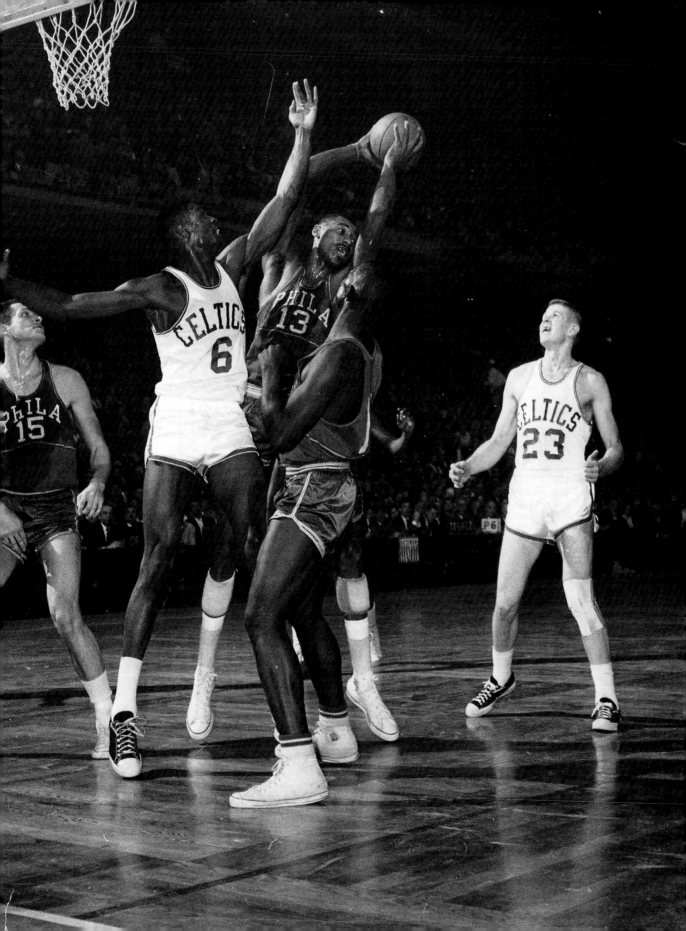

The 100-Point Game

Although the Boston Celtics won the NBA Championship in 1962, Wilt Chamberlain of the Philadelphia Warriors enjoyed the most remarkable season any player has ever had in the NBA.

Chamberlain averaged an NBA record 50.4 points per game and became the only player to surpass 4,000 points in one season with 4,029. He also led the league in rebounding with 25.7 per game and was second in field-goal percentage at .506.

That same year, Chamberlain averaged 48.5 minutes per game—an amazing feat considering that an NBA game only lasts 48 minutes. The Warriors played 10 overtime periods in 7 games that season. Chamberlain was on the court 3,882 out of 3,890 minutes. Of the team's 80 games, Chamberlain played every second in a record 79 of them. But nothing compared to his performance against the New York Knicks on March 2, 1962.

In that game, Chamberlain scored 23 points in the first quarter. That was a lot of points even by his standards, and few thought he could keep up the pace the entire game. Just to make sure that he didn't, New York put two men on Chamberlain and held him to 18 points in the second quarter. Still, the 41-point effort by halftime was impressive, and Chamberlain had a shot at breaking his NBA-best 78 points in 1 game.

In the third quarter, something amazing happened: Chamberlain poured in 28 points. Now he had 69 with 1 quarter remaining. Reaching 78 seemed like a breeze. Could he possibly score 100 points?

Chamberlain's teammates were eager to see their star shine. They continually fed him the ball. Despite New York's stall tactics, Chamberlain broke his single-game scoring mark 40 minutes into the game. Now all he could think about was the 100-point barrier.

Unfortunately for Chamberlain, he hit a 2-minute scoring drought late in the game. Unwilling to lose his chance at scoring immortality, Chamberlain played with more determination than ever. With just 46 seconds remaining in the game, Chamberlain scored his 100th point on a thunderous dunk. His 100-point game has remained one of the most amazing feats in NBA history—one which will stand for a long, long time.

Wilt Chamberlain holds a sign after scoring 100 points in 1 game.

The Celtics Win Eight in a Row

The Boston Celtics had fought off the challenge of the 76ers in the previous year's Eastern Division Finals, but Philadelphia was ready to cause more problems for Boston in the 1965-66 season. Rookie forward Billy Cunningham made an immediate impact. Joining Wilt Chamberlain, Chet Walker, and Lucious Jackson up front, Cunningham averaged 14.3 points per game. Hal Greer and Wali Jones manned the backcourt.

During the season, the 76ers beat the Celtics 6 times in 10 meetings. They eventually won 55 games and took the Eastern Division title away from the Celtics for the first time in 10 years. Chamberlain led the league in scoring for the last time, averaging 33.5 points per game and passing Bob Pettit as the NBA's all-time leading scorer.

The playoffs were a different story. Coach Red Auerbach had announced his retirement after the end of the season. The Celtics wanted to give him one last championship.

Boston defeated Cincinnati in five games to set up the match with Philadelphia. The 76ers were rusty from their two-week layoff, and the Celtics beat them in five games.

The Los Angeles Lakers won their seven-game Western Finals series over the Hawks to meet Boston for the champion-

ship. The Lakers took the opener in overtime in Boston, but the Celtics won the next three. Though L.A. fought back to tie the series, Boston won the final game to give Auerbach his eighth straight NBA title. It was the longest championship streak in NBA history—and established the Celtics as the NBA's all-time greatest basketball dynasty.

The Celtics battle it out at the Boston Garden in the 1966 NBA playoffs.

Willis Reed and the Knicks

The 1970 NBA Finals went down in NBA history as one of the most exciting ever played because of one man: New York Knicks' center Willis Reed.

Reed had been dominating the injury-plagued Wilt Chamberlain of the Lakers. But then Reed tore a leg muscle in Game 5, tipping the balance in favor of Los Angeles. The Knicks used undersized players to slow Chamberlain down, and hung on to win that game. But with Reed out of Game 6, Chamberlain was unstoppable as he scored 45 points to tie the series. Without Reed in the game, the Knicks were doomed.

Minutes before the start of Game 7 in New York, the Knicks left the locker room convinced that their starting center could not play. Just before tip-off, Reed limped onto the court. Madison Square Garden erupted. The Knicks had their leader back.

Reed scored New York's first two baskets and battled Chamberlain the entire game. His heroic play inspired his teammates, who went on to a 113-99 victory. For his efforts, Reed was named the Finals' Most Valuable Player.

Opposite page: Willis Reed of the New York Knickerbockers.

Kareem and the Milwaukee Bucks

During the 1969-1970 season, rookie center Lew Alcindor led the Milwaukee Bucks to a 56-26 record before bowing out of the playoffs in the second round. Great things were expected of the Bucks the following season—and to make sure of it, Milwaukee signed All-Star guard Oscar Robertson. Now the Bucks had a balanced attack with which they could seek a championship.

Alcindor changed his name to Kareem Abdul-Jabbar, then went out and destroyed the competition. Milwaukee finished with an impressive 66-16 record and set 6 NBA records, including 34 home wins, 28 road wins, and a 20-game winning streak. Kareem led the league in scoring with a 31.7 average and was named the NBA's Most Valuable Player.

Milwaukee had little trouble in the playoffs, defeating San Francisco and Los Angeles to reach the finals against the Baltimore Bullets. Baltimore could not stop Abdul-Jabbar and Robertson and were swept for the championship. In only their third season, Milwaukee had become the class of their league—faster than any other expansion club in the history of professional sports.

Kareem Abdul-Jabbar shoots his sky-hook for the Milwaukee Bucks.

The Lakers' Streak

Even though the Lakers' Elgin Baylor was one of the most dominating players of his time, his team had never been able to beat the Boston Celtics in the NBA Finals. Nine games into the 1971-72 season, he decided to retire. With Wilt Chamberlain and Jerry West coming to the end of their careers, the Lakers decided to get forwards Jim McMillian and Happy Hairston and guard Gail Goodrich to help their aging stars.

The result was amazing. From November 5 to January 7, the Lakers went on a league-record 33-game winning streak. Even more, Los Angeles posted a 69-13 record—at the time, the best one-season record in NBA history. Chamberlain led the league in field-goal percentage (.649) and rebounding (19.2), while Goodrich (25.9) and West (25.8) did most of the scoring.

The Lakers swept the Chicago Bulls in four straight. Then against Milwaukee, Chamberlain got the best of Kareem Abdul-Jabbar as Los Angeles won in six games. The Lakers faced the New York Knicks in the championship series. Without center Willis Reed, they were no match for Los Angeles, who finally got their championship in five games.

Opposite page:
Wilt Chamberlain (13) grabs a
rebound while playing for the
Lakers.

A Golden Season

In 1974, experts agreed that the Washington Bullets were the team to beat. They had experience and talent, with powerful Elvin Hayes and Wes Unseld up front and sharpshooter Phil Chenier in the backcourt.

But in the Western Conference, the Golden State Warriors felt they had a championship-caliber team—and they wanted to prove it. Led by high-scoring forward Rick Barry, young center Clifford Ray, and forward Keith Wilkes, the Warriors won 48 games to earn the conference title.

In the playoffs, Golden State defeated Seattle in six games, then stunned a talented Chicago Bulls team in seven games to reach the Finals against the heavily-favored Bullets.

Most observers felt the Warriors' luck had finally run out. But Golden State stunned the basketball world by winning four straight games to post only the third sweep in the 29-year history of the NBA Finals.

"It has to be the greatest upset in the history of the NBA Finals," Rick Barry said. "It was like a fairy-tale season. Everything just fell into place. It's something I'll treasure the rest of my life."

Golden State forward Rick Barry (dark uniform) goes in for a lay-up against Atlanta.

Portland's Championship Season

When the 1976-77 NBA season began, few thought the Portland Trail Blazers had much of a chance to reach the playoffs, let alone the NBA finals. In 1976, Portland finished last in their division, and the team seemed to be in turmoil. Their star center, Bill Walton, was often injured. Fans were getting impatient with him.

But Walton remained healthy for most of the 1976-77 season. As a result, the Blazers finished with a 49-33 mark—good for second place in the Pacific Division. More importantly, they were in the playoffs for the first time in their short history.

The playoffs were considered a bonus for Portland. They were not expected to go far. In the first round, they struggled with the Chicago Bulls—but won the series 2-1. Then they defeated the Denver Nuggets 4-2 to reach the Western Division Finals. Standing in their way were the powerful Los Angeles Lakers and their star center, Kareem Abdul-Jabbar. Certainly this dream season was about to end—or was it?

In the most shocking series of them all, Portland swept the Lakers 4-0 to reach the NBA Championship series. Now even the NBA title seemed possible. But it would have to come against superstar Julius Erving and the Philadelphia 76ers.

Portland lost the first two games. It looked as if they had finally met their match. But the Trail Blazers refused to quit. With one last amazing effort, they beat the 76ers in the next four games. Portland's championship was one of the most amazing upsets in NBA history.

Bill Walton (32) of the Portland Trail Blazers.

Magic Johnson Fills In

Los Angeles Lakers center Kareem Abdul-Jabbar hadn't won an NBA title since 1971 with the Milwaukee Bucks. So when his team reached the Finals in 1980, he wasn't about to let the opportunity slip by. Kareem dominated the 1980 Finals as rookie forward Earvin "Magic" Johnson fed him the ball in the first five games. But then tragedy struck. Abdul-Jabbar badly twisted an ankle in Game 5 and couldn't make the trip to Philadelphia for Game 6.

With nothing to lose, the Lakers played loose at the Spectrum. Jamaal Wilkes played one of his best games ever and finished with 37 points.

But Magic Johnson was the big news. Starting at center for the injured Abdul-Jabbar, Johnson eventually played every position while scoring 42 points. His most devastating shot was the hook shot, which Kareem had used to perfection. Even more, Johnson had 15 rebounds and 7 assists as the Lakers wrapped up the title.

Opposite page: Earvin "Magic" Johnson (dark uniform) goes up against the Chicago Bulls in his rookie season.

Dr. J and Moses

When Julius Erving came to Philadelphia for the 1976-77 season, experts predicted that a new dynasty would be born. While the 76ers made three trips to the Finals in Erving's first six years with the team, they had never won a championship. That all changed in 1982 when center Moses Malone joined the team.

That same season, the 76ers finished with a 65-17 record and captured the Atlantic Division title. In the playoffs, they swept the New York Knicks and defeated Milwaukee in five games. Now they were in the Finals against Magic Johnson and the Los Angeles Lakers.

Everyone talked about the Erving-Johnson matchup. But the real difference was Moses Malone. The 76ers shocked the NBA when they completed a 4-game sweep over Los Angeles. Just as impressive, the 76ers had streaked through the play-offs with a 12-1 record—one of the most dominating performances in NBA playoff history.

Opposite page: Moses Malone and Julius Erving (6) dominate the offense for the Sixers.

The Lakers Stun Boston

Wilt Chamberlain had been on two NBA Championship teams. Jerry West earned his championship ring in 1972. But none of the Laker greats had known the thrill of beating the Boston Celtics in the NBA Finals.

Only the St. Louis Hawks in 1958 had ever beaten the Celtics in the Finals. Boston then went on to win eight straight titles. Except for the 1958 championship, the other 15 times the Celtics had made it to the Finals, they came away with the title.

The Finals streak came to an end in 1985. And it took two of the NBA's all-time greats—Kareem Abdul-Jabbar and Magic Johnson—to accomplish the task. The Lakers won two of three games in Boston, including the Game 6 finale.

"All of our skeletons are out of the closet," said Lakers' coach Pat Riley. "I don't want to hear about history anymore. The history is this: This was our year. And we did it on the parquet floor. Maybe that's the ultimate test."

Opposite page: Kareem Abdul-Jabbar
and the Lakers dominate in 1985.

1986

Boston's Home Cookin'

Boston's Larry Bird won his second consecutive Most Valuable Player Award in 1985. But losing to the Los Angeles Lakers in the NBA Finals ruined his season. So, Bird was determined to lead the Celtics back to the top.

In 1986, Bird finished in the NBA's Top 10 in 5 categories: scoring (25.8 points per game), rebounding (9.8 rebounds per game), steals (2.02), freethrow percentage (.896) and three-point field-goal percentage (.423).

As a team, the Celtics made an important acquisition. Bill Walton came from the Los Angeles Clippers in a trade for Cedric Maxwell. Though plagued by injuries for years, Walton surprised everyone by playing a career-high 80 games, backing up Robert Parish and Kevin McHale.

Boston finished with a franchise-best 67-15 record—including an amazing 40-1 home record. In the playoffs, the Celtics swept the Chicago Bulls, defeated the Atlanta Hawks in five games, then swept the Milwaukee Bucks to reach the NBA Finals against Ralph Sampson and Hakeem Olajuwon of the Houston Rockets.

Playing at the top of his game, Bird averaged 24.0 points, 9.7 rebounds, and 9.5 assists. He also led Boston's defense against Olajuwon and Sampson as the Celtics took the series in six games to win its record-16th title.

Celtics players celebrate after winning the 1986 championship.

Michael's Scoring Tear

Since Wilt Chamberlain's record-breaking scoring efforts in the early 1960s, the NBA had not seen a dominating offensive performance until the 1986-87 season.

Chicago's Michael Jordan, who had missed most of the previous season with a broken foot, gave the NBA a taste of things to come when he returned to score 63 points against the Boston Celtics in a playoff game.

Now fully healthy for the 1986-87 season, Jordan tore through the league with a vengeance. He scored 3,041 points for a 37.1 points per game average and his first NBA scoring title. It was the first time a player had topped the 3,000-point mark since Chamberlain in 1963, and the third-highest total in NBA history. Jordan went on to win seven consecutive scoring titles, matching Chamberlain's record-seven straight titles from 1960 to 1966.

Opposite page: Michael Jordan (23) celebrates with a teammate after scoring against the Celtics, 1987.

Larry Bird
Steals the Show

The Boston Celtics were one of the best teams in the 1980s. With Larry Bird leading the way, the Celtics won three NBA championships. But in 1987, the Detroit Pistons and their star guard Isiah Thomas wanted to prove that they were the NBA's best.

The Pistons got their chance to prove themselves in the Eastern Conference Finals against Boston. They played Boston tough, and in Game 5, they held a one-point lead—and the ball—with only five seconds remaining in the game. A victory—which seemed certain—would give them a 3-2 series lead heading back to Detroit where they could clinch the conference title.

But then Larry Bird came up with one of the most amazing plays in playoff history. Thomas inbounded the ball toward teammate Bill Laimbeer. But Bird anticipated the pass. In one continuous motion, he leaped in front of Laimbeer, stole the ball, and passed it to teammate Dennis Johnson. Johnson's shot at the buzzer was good, and the Celtics won the game. Boston went on to win the series in seven games and claim the Eastern Conference title.

Larry Bird (33) dribbles down the court.

Two in a Row

No NBA team had won back-to-back championships since the Boston Celtics did it in 1968 and 1969. Many believed that the league's expansion had spread the talent so thin that repeating had become nearly impossible. Lakers' coach Pat Riley was not among the believers.

Though the Lakers had won four championships in the 1980s, Riley was not satisfied with his team's position as the "Team of the '80s." If the Lakers could win back-to-back championships, they would be considered one of the all-time greats. A day after their 1987 Finals victory, Riley guaranteed the Lakers would repeat.

In the 1987-88 season, the Lakers notched the NBA's best record at 62-20. Byron Scott and James Worthy shared the scoring load with Kareem Abdul-Jabbar and Magic Johnson.

But the talent did not stop there. The Lakers' bench was deep. Mychal Thompson shared the center spot with Abdul-Jabbar. Third-year forward A. C. Green and veterans Michael Cooper and Kurt Rambis made important contributions.

As the Lakers set their sights on another championship, a new challenger loomed in the East. The Detroit Pistons had won 54 games and the Central Division. They had surrounded superstar guard Isiah Thomas with tough rebounders Bill Laimbeer and Rick Mahorn, scorers Adrian Dantley, Joe Dumars and Vinnie Johnson, and aggressive defensive forwards Dennis Rodman and John Salley.

In the Finals, Detroit put Los Angeles to the test. Using home-court advantage, the Lakers came back from a 3-2 deficit to win the final two games in the Forum. In doing so, the Lakers became the first repeat champions since the 1968-69 Boston Celtics.

Lakers forward James Worthy (42) passes the ball down court.

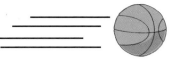

Repeat Pistons

Before the start of the 1989-90 season, the NBA champion Detroit Pistons looked to join Boston and Los Angeles as the only teams to win back-to-back titles.

Detroit won 59 games and their third straight Central Division title. But standing in the way were the Chicago Bulls, who had built a solid team around Michael Jordan, and who had won 55 games under new coach Phil Jackson.

In the playoffs, Detroit had little trouble with Indiana and New York. But the Pistons needed seven games to defeat the Bulls. Nevertheless, Detroit had made it to the Finals again. This time, they would face the underdog Portland Trail Blazers. A repeat championship seemed like a sure thing.

But Portland won Game 2 in Detroit by one point in overtime. That amazing victory tied the Finals at 1-1. Now the young and talented Blazers seemed ready to score a major upset.

That's when the veteran Pistons took over. Behind Isiah Thomas' 27.6 points per game, Detroit took three straight games in Portland to capture a second straight title. After going 19 years without back-to-back champions, the NBA now had back-to-back repeaters.

The Detroit Pistons' bench celebrates in the closing minutes of the NBA Finals.

The Bulls' Three-peat

From 1988-89 to 1991-92, the Phoenix Suns had won 50 or more games 4 straight years. The Suns had guards Kevin Johnson and Jeff Hornacek, and forwards Tom Chambers and Dan Majerle. Phoenix was a regular visitor to the playoffs.

But making the playoffs wasn't good enough. Three days after the 1992 Finals ended, the Suns traded Hornacek, starting forward Tim Perry, and backup center Andrew Lang to Philadelphia for superstar Charles Barkley.

Immediately, the Suns challenged for the NBA title. They won a league-best 62 games, then beat the Lakers, San Antonio, and Seattle to make it to the Finals.

Meanwhile, the defending champion Chicago Bulls set their sights on a third straight NBA Championship. They coasted through the regular season with 57 wins, but lost home-court advantage in the playoffs to the New York Knicks. Meeting in the Eastern Conference Finals, the two teams split the first four games, the home team winning each time. Then the Bulls won Game 5 in New York before clinching the series in Chicago in Game 6.

Phoenix had a good chance to win the title. They had home court advantage throughout the Finals. But the Bulls won the first two games in Phoenix. Heading back to Chicago, the Bulls

looked as though they would sweep their way to another championship. But the Suns won two of three in Chicago before losing in Game 6 at home.

With the win, the Bulls became only the third team in NBA history to win as many as three consecutive championships, joining Boston (1959-66) and Minneapolis (1952-54).

Michael Jordan celebrates after the Bulls win their third NBA title, 1993.

Mr. Robinson's Scoring Title

Center David Robinson of the San Antonio Spurs won the scoring championship in 1994. But the title wasn't wrapped up until the final game of the season.

Orlando Magic center Shaquille O'Neal led Robinson by an average of .06 points going into the last game. Robinson played earlier in the day against the Los Angeles Clippers.

The Clippers committed 28 fouls, most of them against Robinson in an attempt to slow him down. But Robinson's teammates helped him by continually feeding him the ball.

As a result, Robinson scored a career-high 71 points. He finished the season with 2,383 points in 80 games, giving him an average of 29.787 per game. That meant O'Neal needed 68 against the New Jersey Nets that night to win the scoring title. But he had only 32 and finished with a 29.346 average.

Robinson's 71 points established a team record, surpassing George Gervin's 63 on April 9, 1978. It was one of the most amazing scoring efforts in NBA history.

Opposite page: Center David Robinson of the San Antonio Spurs won the scoring championship in 1994.

Hakeem's Dream Season

Hakeem Olajuwon had always been the NBA's most un-derrated superstar. It was flashy players like Magic Johnson, Larry Bird, Michael Jordan, Isiah Thomas, and Charles Barkley who captured the spotlight. In 1986, Olajuwon made it to the NBA Finals in only his second NBA season. But after losing to the Celtics, his team did not return to the championship game until 1994. That year, Olajuwon not only won his first MVP Award, he brought the city of Houston its first major-league championship in any professional sport.

Olajuwon was unstoppable in the NBA Finals. He outdueled New York's Patrick Ewing and scored 26.9 points per game despite his team's 86.1 points per game average. Olajuwon also averaged 9.1 rebounds, 3.6 assists, and 3.86 blocked shots. It was Olajuwon's block of John Starks' desperation three-pointer that earned Houston's 86-84 win in Game 6.

Finally in the spotlight, Olajuwon added a championship ring and the NBA Finals MVP Award to his regular-season MVP trophy. The following year, with former Houston teammate Clyde Drexler at his side, Olajuwon would lead the Rockets to their second-straight NBA title.

Opposite page: Center Hakeem Olajuwon (34) dunks the ball over New York Knicks center Patrick Ewing.

The Greatest
Team Ever?

Before the 1995-96 season, Chicago Bulls' superstar guard Michael Jordan seemed to be at the crossroads. He had just come off an ill-fated attempt at a baseball career, followed by a disappointing NBA season in which he did not win the scoring title, nor the championship. For the first time, people wondered if Jordan's abilities were slipping.

In 1995-96, Jordan answered his critics by leading the Chicago Bulls to one of the most remarkable seasons in NBA history.

It all began with the acquisition of defensive forward Dennis Rodman of the San Antonio Spurs. Rodman was the tough rebounder the Bulls needed to make a run at the championship. Once he was signed, the Bulls were favored to win it all.

Chicago started the year 23-2, then set their sights on an NBA-record 70 victories. Not only did they reach 70, they passed it, finishing the season with an amazing 72-10 record—topping the 69-13 mark of the 1972 Los Angeles Lakers.

So now the debate was on: Were the 1995-96 Chicago Bulls the greatest team ever? Experts and fans wanted to see how the Bulls performed in the playoffs before they decided.

Chicago knocked off the Miami Heat and the New York Knicks, then swept Shaquille O'Neal and the Orlando Magic to

**Michael Jordan goes up against
Shaquille O'Neal in the 1996 playoffs.**

reach the Finals. Standing in their way to basketball immortality was Shawn Kemp and the Seattle SuperSonics.

The Bulls took the first two games in Chicago, then embarrassed the SuperSonics in Seattle in Game 3. It looked like a sweep was at hand, but then Seattle won the next two games to put the championship in doubt. Back in Chicago for Game 6, the Bulls ended any speculation that they were about to choke by defeating Seattle for the title.

Jordan became the first player to win the NBA Finals Most Valuable Player Award four times. Since the award was first given out in 1969, only Jordan and former Los Angeles Lakers' star Magic Johnson had won it three times.

Jordan and Scottie Pippen collected their fourth NBA titles. Rodman, John Salley and James Edwards — all members of the 1989 and 1990 champion Detroit Pistons—earned their third.

Chicago's Phil Jackson became just the fourth coach in league history to win four titles. Red Auerbach won nine with the Boston Celtics in the 1950s and 1960s, John Kundla captured five with the Minneapolis Lakers in the 1940s and 1950s, and Pat Riley won four with the Los Angeles Lakers in the 1980s.

With the championship win, the debate resumed. Were the 1995-96 Bulls the greatest team ever? Critics pointed to the two losses in the Finals and the "diluted" talent against whom the Bulls played all season long. But no one can argue this fact: Chicago's 72-10 regular-season record is the all-time greatest—and may stand for decades to come.

Opposite page: Michael Jordan won his record-fourth NBA Finals Most Valuable Player Award in 1996.

More Unforgettable Moments

1948—Washington wins 15 consecutive games at the start of the season.

1950—Rochester wins 15 consecutive games at the end of the season.

1953—Bob Cousy sinks 30 free throws in 1 playoff game.

1958—Bill Russell hauls down 40 rebounds in 1 playoff game.

1959—Bob Cousy records 19 assists in 1 half.

1960—Wilt Chamberlain grabs 55 rebounds in 1 game.

Bob Cousy (14) of the Boston Celtics.

1960—Boston hauls down 109 rebounds in 1 game.

1962—Syracuse scores 50 points in the first quarter against San Francisco.

1962—Elgin Baylor scores 284 points in a 7-game playoff series; also scores 61 points in a Finals game.

1965—Rookie Rick Barry scores 57 points in 1 game.

1965—Nate Thurmond snatches 18 rebounds in 1 quarter.

1965—Jerry West scores 278 points in a 6-game playoff series.

1966—Wilt Chamberlain leads the league in scoring for the seventh time in his career.

1966—Jerry West sinks 840 free throws in 1 season.

1967—Wilt Chamberlain hauls down 41 rebounds in 1 playoff game.

1968—Rookie Earl Monroe scores 56 points in 1 game.

1972—Los Angeles defeats Golden State by 63 points (162-99).

1973—Wilt Chamberlain hauls down his 23,924th career rebound.

1973—Elmore Smith blocks 17 shots in 1 game.

Earl Monroe (33) scores for the Bullets.

1973—Tiny Archibald wins the NBA scoring title.

1974—Boston snatches 61 defensive rebounds in 1 game.

1975—Kareem Abdul-Jabbar hauls down 29 defensive rebounds in 1 game.

1975—Golden State steals the ball 25 times in 1 game.

1975—Dave Cowens hauls down 20 defensive rebounds in 1 playoff game.

1976—Kareem Abdul-Jabbar snatches 1,111 defensive rebounds in 1 season.

1976—Quinn Buckner records eight steals in one half.

1976—Larry Kenon records 11 steals in 1 game.

1977—Moses Malone snatches 15 offensive rebounds in 1 playoff game.

1978—David Thompson scores 73 points in 1 game.

1978—George Gervin scores 33 points in 1 quarter.

1978—Milwaukee wins eight overtime games in one season.

1979—Moses Malone hauls down 587 offensive rebounds in 1 season.

1981—Kareem Abdul-Jabbar records his 9th season with 2,000 or more points.

1981—Calvin Murphy records a .958 free throw percentage in one season.

1982—Moses Malone snatches 21 offensive rebounds in 1 game.

1982—Denver averages 126.5 points per game.

1982—Boston scores 50 points in the first quarter against Denver.

1982—Utah scores 50 points in the first quarter against Denver.

1983—Randy Smith plays in his 906th consecutive game.

1983—Detroit scores 186 points in 1 game.

1984—John Lucas records 14 assists in 1 quarter.

1984—Magic Johnson records 24 assists in 1 playoff game.

1985—Mark Eaton blocks 456 shots in 1 season; also blocks 10 shots in 1 playoff game.

1985—Boston scores 148 points in 1 NBA Finals game.

1986—Alvin Robertson records 301 steals in 1 season.

Charles Barkley slam dunks the ball.

1987—Charles Barkley snatches 13 offensive rebounds in 1 half.

1988—John Stockton records 24 assists in 1 playoff game.

1988—Hakeem Olajuwon scores 150 points in a 4-game playoff series.

1988—Michael Jordan scores 226 points in a 5-game playoff series.

1989—Kareem Abdul-Jabbar plays in his 20th season and 1,560th career game; also scores his 38,387th career point and 3,189th career blocked shot.

1989—Golden State records 25 steals in 1 game.

1989—Milwaukee scores 50 points in the first quarter against Orlando.

1989—Sacramento sinks 16 three-point field goals in one game.

Hakeem Olajuwon drives to the basket.

1989—Michael Jordan sinks 23 free throws in 1 playoff game.

1989—Los Angeles wins 11 consecutive playoff games.

1990—Scott Skiles records 30 assists in 1 game.

1990—Phoenix scores 107 points in the first half against Denver.

1990—Phoenix sinks 61 free throws in 1 game.

1990—Boston scores 157 points in 1 playoff game.

1991—John Stockton records 1,164 assists in 1 season.

1991—Cleveland defeats Miami by 68 points (148-80).

1991—New Jersey blocks 22 shots in 1 game.

1992—Dennis Rodman averages 18.7 rebounds per game.

1992—Dominique Wilkens sinks 23-of-23 free throws in 1 game.

1992—Michael Jordan scores 135 points in a 3-game playoff series.

1993—Houston wins 15 consecutive games at the start of the season.

1993—Michael Jordan leads the NBA in scoring for the seventh time in his career.

1993—Brian Shaw scores 10 three-point field goals in 1 game.

1993—Michael Williams sinks 84-consecutive free throws in 1 season.

1993—Dan Majerle sinks eight three-point field goals in one playoff game.

1994—Dan Majerle scores 192 three-point field goals in one season.

Michael Jordan flies over the defense for two.

1994—Robert Parish hauls down his 9,599th career defensive rebound.

1994—Phoenix sinks 12 three-point field goals in one playoff game.

1995—Steve Kerr records a 52.4 three-point field goal percentage.

1995—John Stockton becomes the NBA's all-time assist leader and steals leader.

Index

63